WAITING ON

Hope

An Advent Devotional

JOY BANNEN

WESTBOW
PRESS®
A DIVISION OF THOMAS NELSON
& ZONDERVAN

WestBow Press books may be ordered through booksellers or by contacting:

WestBow Press
A Division of Thomas Nelson & Zondervan
1663 Liberty Drive
Bloomington, IN 47403
www.westbowpress.com
844-714-3454

Scripture quotations are from the ESV® Bible (The Holy Bible, English Standard Version®), copyright © 2001 by Crossway, a publishing ministry of Good News Publishers. Used by permission. All rights reserved.

ISBN: 978-1-6642-7392-4 (sc)
ISBN: 978-1-6642-7393-1 (e)

Library of Congress Control Number: 2022913991

Print information available on the last page.

WestBow Press rev. date: 09/21/2022

Introduction

A Celebration of Advent

Waiting is hard! That is one universal truth that people from all walks of life can agree on. We spend much of our lives agonizing over waiting. Waiting on a promotion that will better support a growing family. Waiting to hold a long-desired baby. Waiting on a test result to find out if the latest treatments have worked against a devastating disease. Waiting at the airport for a dearly missed loved one. The irony of waiting is that we live in a fast-paced, fast food, fast-talking world. We live in a society where one does not have to wait for a letter to arrive by post to receive an update on a loved one deployed oceans away; we can call or FaceTime them to talk to them instantly. We do not have to spend hours, and even days, prepping for a holiday meal; we can place an order at a restaurant or grocery store ahead of time to have dinner and all the trimmings delivered to our home. We don't even have to wait in line for the coffee we were too busy to make at home. We can order our three-pump, venti vanilla latte with an extra shot of espresso from our phone on the drive to the coffeehouse, then skip the line, skip the small talk, and go about our day without any wait.

Maybe you grew up celebrating Advent. Maybe you had a family Advent calendar or tradition as a child you still remember. I did not grow up celebrating Christ's birth with Advent. Having a Christmas Eve birthday, I grew up sharing my red velvet birthday cake with Jesus every year. We sang happy birthday to Jesus, and every Christmas morning, before we opened a single present, we sat down with our homemade sausage balls and apple cinnamon tea to listen as our dad read the Christmas story found in Luke 2:1–20.

As an adult with children of my own, I am struck by the fact that Christmas is not about the perfectly decorated trees or neatly wrapped packages under the tree. I did not want my girls spending hours writing their laundry list of toys and other things they wanted. I did not want to drive my family crazy by stressing out over having special meals and forced traditions. I wanted my girls to grow up understanding we do not have Christmas so we can see our second and third cousins once a year or so we can greedily open gift after gift. We have Christmas because the all-powerful creator God loved us so much that He decided to send His one and only Son to earth in the form of an innocent baby. We have Christmas because God sent this perfect infant to live among us, to show God to the world, and, ultimately, to die an agonizing death on a cross meant for a murderer, only to rise again three days later so that we sinful and lost humans could one day live with Him in heaven. *Praise God*! That is something to celebrate! That is something worth anticipating and waiting for!

My husband comes from a Catholic family, and, in our early years of dating, I heard several references to Advent, such as Advent calendars and Advent wreaths. At first, I thought it was a Catholic tradition to countdown to Christmas. However, as I became more aware of the meaning of word advent, I started noticing Protestant Advent devotionals and Advent scripture reading plans. I realized it was not just a tradition for Catholics but an observance for all believers. I discovered a beautiful reminder that was far deeper than just a countdown to opening presents. The word Advent comes from the Latin word *adventus*, which means coming. *Adventus* is a Latin translation of the Greek word parousia, which means the Second Coming as used in Matthew 24:27, "For as the lightning comes from the east and shines as far as the west, so will be the coming of the Son of Man." The purpose behind Advent is to prepare our hearts to celebrate the first Advent of our Savior in the fully human form of a baby, and to prepare our hearts for the anticipated return of Christ, our Lord and King, in the Second Advent.

Our focus in this season is crucial. The world is sending constant signals to distract us from the true purpose of Christmas. The ads and decorations start going up as early as Halloween in some stores. Our eyes are pulled from the baby Jesus by early Black Friday deals and secret Cyber Monday specials. Our attention is turned away from anticipating the Second Advent of our Savior by thoughts and plans of getting together with in-laws and other extended family and friends. We are easily distracted by long to-do lists and dozens upon dozens of "holiday" cards. (Because even saying "Merry Christmas" has now become offensive during the *Christ*mas season, but that's another topic for another time.)

This devotional is organized to follow the order of the candles in an Advent wreath, which has five candles. Four candles sit around the outside, and one candle sits in the center. The four outside candles represent hope, preparation (some traditions say peace), joy, and love. The candle in the center represents Christ. Tradition states that you light one of the outside candles each Sunday before Christmas, starting four Sundays before Christmas. The first Sunday you light the hope candle; the second Sunday you relight the hope candle, and then light the preparation candle; and so on. Then on Christmas day, you relight all four of the outside candles, and, at last, you light the Christ candle in the center. With that in mind, we will spend five days reflecting on each candle. As you read through these paragraphs and scriptures to prepare your home and yourself for Christmas, keep the following questions in the forefront of your mind: How will my anticipation of the Second Coming of Christ affect my focus this Christmas season? How can Advent help me keep the focus on Christ my Savior this season? Is Christ the center of my life?

Let's celebrate the birth of Christ and the Second Coming of our Savior together!

Behold, I am coming soon. (Revelation 22:7a)

Week 1

Hope

Week 1

Hope

In hope he [Abraham] believed against hope, that he should become the father of many nations, as he had been told, "So shall your offspring be." He did not weaken in faith when he considered his own body, which was as good as dead (since he was about a hundred years old), or when he considered the barrenness of Sarah's womb. No unbelief made him waver concerning the promise of God, but he grew strong in his faith as he gave glory to God, fully convinced that God was able to do what he had promised. That is why his faith was "counted to him as righteousness."

—Romans 4:18–22

A braham is an exemplary figure in the scripture of the strength one gains through faith and hope. He had realized by the ripe old age of one hundred that his faith and hope for things not yet seen brought glory to God. In an article titled [1]"Faith: In Hope, against Hope, for the Glory of God," John Piper says, "Faith gives God glory because it shows that God can and will do the great, necessary good that humans can't do." Abraham held onto the hope that God's promises were real, and that God would fulfill what He promised. He did not allow

---

[1] John Piper, "Faith: In Hope, against Hope for the Glory of God," 9/6/1999, https://www.desiringgod.org/messages/faith-in-hope-against-hope-for-the-glory-of-god.

his old age and his wife's barrenness deter his hope that God *could* and *would* fulfill His promises to Abraham of having a son. Unfortunately, the Israelites did not hold on to this strong faith and lost their hope.

Through prophets, inspired by God, the Israelites had been promised a Messiah. A Messiah, an eternal King, who would save them, lead them, and rule over them forever. Yet when it did not happen when and how they expected, they doubted and turned to their own old ways. They stopped listening to God, and, eventually, God stopped talking to them. Insert Mary and the angel Gabriel.

Four hundred years later, in a tiny town of Nazareth, Mary was greeted by the angel Gabriel, and her life was forever changed because she dared to hope. When Mary went to share with her cousin, Elizabeth, what she had just seen and heard, Elizabeth was immediately filled with the spirit and proclaimed, "And blessed is she who believed that there would be a fulfillment of what was spoken to her from the Lord" (Luke 1:45). Elizabeth was holding on to some hope of her own. She was steadfast in her hope that even though she had been barren all these years, God *could* and *would* give her the son He'd promised, and that son would bring [2]"joy and gladness" to her and her husband, Zechariah.

These poignant examples of a life lived in hope point us toward how Christians today are to live in this generation that is marked by the tension of the "already-but-not-yet" hope. As God's children, we *already know* that Christ is returning. We *already know* that God has overcome sin and death and given us victory through His death and resurrection. However, we do not always live well in the tension of *knowing* that has happened and *believing* Christ Jesus will literally return to this earth again one day to bring His children home to Him as He promises in His Word. It has been almost two thousand years since Christ's sandal last left an imprint on the dirt of this earth. Modern-day believers are so far removed from the resurrection; we do not live life with our eyes constantly on the skies, waiting expectantly for our Savior to come through the clouds. As modern-day believers, we are living for our own personal pleasure, we are striving in our own strength, *until* … -Until a mother has to bury her

---

[2] Luke 1:14 ESV

baby. Until a man walks into an elementary school and murders twenty innocent children. Until a man unexpectedly leaves his wife and children for another woman. Until a hurricane wipes out an entire string of island nations, leaving thousands destitute. *Then* we beg for hope. Then the world cries for something to hope in. Then believers wake up from their fog of egotism and cling to the hope they always knew was there but arrogantly chose to ignore.

As natural disasters destroy homes and consume the lives of many, the earth hopes for the Creator God. As innocent children are forced into human slavery, we hope for the unconditional love and protection of a Father. As nations war with each other, killing anyone who sits in the way of their domination, the world hopes for the one true King who will reign the world in truth and justice. In Romans 8:22–23, Paul writes of this already-but-not-yet hope: "For we know that the whole creation has been groaning together in the pains of childbirth until now. And not only the creation, but we ourselves, who have the first fruits of the Spirit, groan inwardly as we wait eagerly for adoption as sons, the redemption of our bodies."

How Does This Apply to Today's Believers?

This hope for restoration is felt so desperately in our relationships with one another, and specifically in our families. Have you noticed that life seems to happen in waves? First, there's the wave of dating, when our friends start coupling off; they have less time for the group, and more time is spent with the significant other. Then comes the wave of marriage: wedding showers, bachelor/bachelorette parties, wedding gifts, and so forth. Followed by the wave of babies: baby showers, diaper showers, meals to the new mom, and on it goes. Then the *long* wave of children's parties: birthday parties, class parties, fall harvest parties, celebrations of all kinds. Sadly, in the midst of this last wave, comes a new subwave: the divorce wave.

[3]According to a report released in May 2011 by the United States Census Bureau, the average length of American marriages before ending in divorce or separation is 8 years. The numbers get worse when broken down into age categories. Twenty out of every one thousand women who get married between the ages of twenty-five and twenty-nine end up divorced or separated. Compare this to only eighteen in every one thousand women who get married between the ages of thirty-five and thirty-nine and end up divorced or separated. The numbers are not so kind for couples who cohabitate—and let's not fool ourselves by thinking Christian couples never cohabitate. Couples who cohabitate before marriage are three to five times more likely to separate than couples who did not cohabitate before marriage. Our marriages are a mess!

[4]According to a study done by the Barna Group in February 2017, couples who identify as born-again believers had a 32 percent divorce rate. Couples who did not identify as born-again believers but identified themselves as Christians had a 33 percent divorce rate. (The national average divorce rate for America is 41 percent.) [5]George Barna, who directed a similar study in 2008, said, "There no longer seems to be much of a stigma attached to divorce; it is now seen as an unavoidable rite of passage." Believers, *this should not be!* Our families are not "doomed to be torn apart by divorce." We have hope! Our hope is our Redeemer who came to this world over two thousand years ago in the form of a tiny, newborn baby, and *He is coming again!*

> Blessed be the God and Father of our Lord Jesus Christ!
> According to his great mercy, he has caused us to be
> born again to a living hope through the resurrection

---

[3] Rose M. Kreider and Renee Ellis, "Number, Timing, and Duration of Marriages and Divorces: 2009," 5/11, https://www2.census.gov/library/publications/2011/demo/p70-125.pdf.

[4] "The Trends Redefining Romance Today," 2/9/17, https://www.barna.com/research/trends-redefining-romance-today.

[5] "New Marriage and Divorce Statistics Released," 3/31/08, https://www.barna.com/research/new-marriage-and-divorce-statistics-released.

of Jesus Christ from the dead, to an inheritance that is imperishable, undefiled, and unfading, kept in heaven for you, who by God's power are being guarded through faith for a salvation ready to be revealed in the last time. (1 Peter 1:3-5)

Suggested Reading

Suggested Daily Readings

As you read, keep these questions in the back of your mind: How does anticipating the hope of a coming Savior alter your focus? How can you work to keep your focus on the hope we have in Christ during the Christmas season? Spend time reflecting on these verses, and jot down notes in the space below. Come up with a plan for how you will stay intentionally focused on the true reason for Christmas.

Day 1—Psalm 24:1–10

_____
_____
_____
_____
_____
_____
_____
_____
_____
_____
_____
_____
_____
_____
_____
_____

Day 2—Isaiah 61:1–11

_____
_____
_____
_____
_____
_____
_____
_____
_____
_____
_____
_____
_____
_____
_____

Day 3—Malachi 3:1–6

_____
_____
_____
_____
_____
_____
_____
_____
_____
_____
_____
_____
_____
_____
_____

Day 4—Malachi 4:1–5; Isaiah 9:1–7

_____
_____
_____
_____
_____
_____
_____
_____
_____
_____
_____
_____
_____
_____
_____
_____
_____
_____
_____

Day 5—Revelation 21:1–7

_____
_____
_____
_____
_____
_____
_____
_____
_____
_____
_____
_____
_____
_____
_____
_____
_____
_____
_____

Week 2

Preparation

Week 2

Preparation

Jesus said to him, "Have you believed because you have seen me? Blessed are those who have not seen and yet have believed."

—John 20:29

Exodus 29:38–42 details what the Israelites were to offer on the altar: the two lambs, the grain offerings, and the drink offerings. Much preparation went into making these offerings. Numbers 15:22–31 details the laws about unintentional sins. Eight verses are dedicated to detailing how the Israelites were to prepare and make atonement for any sins committed unintentionally. A scant two verses are written to warn that the person who does anything with a "high hand … shall be cut off from among his people" (Numbers 15:30). The Israelites were well familiar with the concept of preparation. They just struggled, as many believers today do, to believe the statement of faith implied by all that preparation.

Preparation is a statement of faith. It is committing to trust even when there is no tangible evidence the thing you are trusting in will come to fruition. Preparation can be committing to trusting, even when we are hurting and heartsick. In faith, we prepare for the birth of a baby, even as our hearts are still healing from the previous loss of two other babies. In faith, we set aside funds for retirement and a family even though we have not yet met the spouse God has for us. In faith, we prepare for a holiday get together even though the doctors have told us our loved one may not live until December 25.

The idea of preparation in Advent is not making sure our to-do lists are complete, our houses are guest ready, and our cards are sent out. For believers, the idea of preparing means spiritually readying our hearts to celebrate the birth of baby Jesus and the imminent coming of Christ to rule once more. Preparation for Advent should include removing distractions and simplifying the holidays. The idea of simplifying distractions is countercultural when applied biblically. Minimalism is the hottest trend right now. I am not suggesting that having a sparsely decorated tree or only wrapping presents in simple brown paper with a string bow will make one any more spiritual than the next person. Yet this idea of removing distractions—cutting back on the commercial side of Christmas—goes against everything we see on TV, hear on the radio, and talk to our coworkers about. How do we apply this? What would it look like; to go against the flow of society and bring the focus of Christmas back to its spiritual origins?

How Do We Prepare for Advent?

In this section you will find three ways to prepare yourselves for Advent this Christmas season. The first way is to stay tightly bound to God's Word. In the final days of his life, Paul reminded his dearly beloved Timothy the importance and usefulness of the Bible. Two Timothy 3:16–17 states, "All Scripture is breathed out by God and profitable for teaching, for reproof, for correction, and for training in righteousness, that the man of God may be competent, equipped for every good work." Finding time to read all of God's Word may feel like an impossibility in these next twenty-five days. Set an alarm, make yourself an appointment, wake up earlier, or stay up a little later. Listen to a podcast or the listen feature of a Bible app as you drive from store to store. Be intentional with your time! When you simplify your holidays and intentionally remove your distractions, finding time to spend in the Word becomes easier. In Psalm 119:9–10, David clearly states, "How can a young man keep his way pure? By guarding it according to your word. With my whole heart I seek you; let me not wander from your commandments!"

David realized his only hope of keeping his way pure was by guarding his steps with God's Word. We must diligently seek God's Word with our *whole* heart, not just half-heartedly to check it off our list. When you are purposeful in your choices, when you cut out some of those empty holiday obligations that have no eternal focus, you free up time to spend with your Savior, thus preparing and guarding your steps. Your family will be better off if, rather than going to that fifth store to get that eighth present, you sit at your kitchen table and spend time reading scripture and praying together about how God can use your marriage and family life for His glory. Be purposeful in the message you are sending to those around you this Christmas. Are you showing them it's more important that you wait in line for forty-five minutes to get an extra 20 percent off that smartwatch they wanted, or that it's more important to spend time at the feet of your Savior?

Another way to prepare ourselves this Christmas season is to look for God's hand. John 1:3 tells believers, "All things were created through Him, and apart from Him not one thing was created that has been created." In our workplaces, we struggle with difficult bosses and negative coworkers. In our families, we are faced with broken relationships, bitterness, and difficult people. Remember that God has seen fit to place these people in your life. Keep Christ your focus by looking for the good in every tough situation. Look for the good in the people involved in each situation you face. Above all, look for the good in God as He allows you to encounter these people and situations every day. In Colossians 1:17, Paul says, "He is before all things, and in him all things hold together." Seek how He would have you bring Him glory in both pleasant and unpleasant interactions. More important than gifts, perfectly prepared meals, or clean homes is our bringing glory to God.

Self-reflection is the third way to preparation. In 1 Thessalonians 5:17, Paul says, "Give thanks in all circumstances; for this is the will of God in Christ Jesus for you." Just as Paul told the church of the Thessalonians, it is God's will for his people to reflect and give thanks. Was this a great year for you or for your career? Rejoice! Praise God for His blessing! Was this a difficult year, marked by sickness, loss, and suffering? Look for God's blessing in that pain. How did He carry you through those difficult days? He may have allowed you to fight through one or two difficult illnesses but have you praised Him for the dozens of other diseases He protected you from this year? Look for ways He has strengthened you and made you a stronger believer. As we prepare our hearts for Christmas day, we are making a statement of faith that we trust that Jesus will return to this earth as He promised.

> And if I go and prepare a place for you, I will come again and will take you to myself, that where I am you may be also. (John 14:3)

> As it is written, "What no eye has seen, nor ear heard, nor the heart of man imagined, what God has prepared for those who love him." (1 Corinthians 2:9)

Suggested Reading

Suggested Daily Readings

As you read, keep these questions in the back of your mind: What distractions can you identify that are keeping you from celebrating Christ this Christmas season? How can you seek to prepare for future challenges? Spend time reflecting on the below verses, and jot down notes in the space provided. Pray and ask God to help you intentionally seek to stay committed to the plan you created for how you will stay focused on the true reason for Christmas.

Day 6—Psalm 80:1–19

_____

_____

_____

_____

_____

_____

_____

_____

_____

_____

_____

_____

_____

_____

_____

_____

_____

Day 7–Matthew 2:1–12

_____
_____
_____
_____
_____
_____
_____
_____
_____
_____
_____
_____
_____
_____
_____
_____
_____

Day 8—Luke 3:1–9

_____
_____
_____
_____
_____
_____
_____
_____
_____
_____
_____
_____
_____
_____
_____
_____
_____

Day 9—Micah 5:1–5

_____
_____
_____
_____
_____
_____
_____
_____
_____
_____
_____
_____
_____
_____
_____
_____

Day 10—Psalm 30:4–6; Isaiah 40:1–3

_____
_____
_____
_____
_____
_____
_____
_____
_____
_____
_____
_____
_____
_____
_____
_____
_____

Week 3

Joy

Week 3

Joy

May the God of hope fill you with all joy and peace in believing, so that by the power of the Holy Spirit you may abound in hope.

—Romans 15:13

Joy is a commonly misunderstood term. The secular world finds the words "joy" and "happiness" interchangeable. However, scripture tells us there is a difference. Happiness is an emotion that is conditional, but joy is not dependent on our circumstances. In 1 Thessalonians 1:6, Paul writes, "And you became imitators of us and of the Lord, for you received the word in much affliction, with the joy of the Holy Spirit." Even though they had received much affliction, the Thessalonians still had the joy of the Holy Spirit. Joy does not come from agreeable circumstances, rather it is a gift from God to His believers. According to Galatians 5:22, joy is the fruit of the Holy Spirit in our lives.

The Greek translation of joy is *chara*, and it can be found in the New Testament. *Chara* is a noun describing a feeling of inner gladness, delight, and rejoicing. This word is not describing a forced emotion resulted from stuffing down pain and pretending it is not there. Instead, this word describes a sense of contentment *despite* present circumstances. Believers can have joy amidst incredible pain because they understand that this world is fleeting. Our time on earth is momentary; we can have joy because we know that every painful day on earth is one day closer to being home in the arms of Jesus. Our joy comes from knowing our bodies may feel physical pain, but our souls are free in Christ. This is why, in 2 Timothy, Paul was able to write to Timothy with such confidence, even though he was in chains and everyone had deserted him. In 2 Timothy 4:8, Paul wrote, "Henceforth there is laid up for me the crown of righteousness, which the Lord, the righteous judge, will award to me on that day, and not only to me but also to all who have loved his appearing."

We have never had to make two sacrifices in a day to atone for our sins. We have never had to make a drink offering, grain offering, or lamb offering for our sins. Every day that we breathe, we take for granted the *free* gift of salvation we enjoy through Christ Jesus. The birth of Jesus is truly the most joyful event to have taken place on earth. His miraculous resurrection would not have happened if He had not first been born in a human body to die in our place.

How to Increase Our Joy

In His Word, God has given us ways to maximize our joy. The first way to is to read God's Word. In John 15:10–11, Jesus tells the disciples, "If you keep my commandments, you will abide in my love, just as I have kept my Father's commandments and abide in his love. These things I have spoken to you, that my joy may be in you, and that your joy may be full." We cannot keep commandments we do not have knowledge of. We *must* read God's Word. In faith-based families, we must read God's Word together. Individual spiritual growth is important, but spiritual growth as a faith-based family is a must. Inevitably, one of you will experience a dry spell while the other remains a sponge, soaking up every word of scripture they read, just glowing with the joy of the Spirit. It is vital to read together so you can encourage each other. When one is struggling to find joy in the pain, the other can be strong and steadily point the way to true and lasting joy. God is the creator of joy; how else can we expect to experience the gift of joy He intends for us if we do not read His life giving words?

The second way is through prayer. In John 16:24, Jesus says to the disciples, "Until now you have asked nothing in my name. Ask, and you will receive, that your joy may be full." You do not ask for a favor from a neighbor with whom you have no relationship. You go to the faithful friend you do have a relationship with and ask them for the favor. Some people will say they don't know how to pray, or that they have never talked to God before. They may tell themselves He doesn't want to hear from them now. Let me be very clear: *God always wants to hear from you.* He is not too busy. He will not answer you with an irritated *what do you want!* Just as we must read God's Word together in our faith-based families, we must pray together and for each other. Does your friend have a tough meeting coming up at work? Cover his day in prayer. Is your sister struggling with patiently and gently correcting her toddler's antics over and over? Cover her words in prayer. Pray with your brothers and sisters over the future. Seek God's will for each other's lives. There is something supernatural that takes place in our hearts when we talk to our Savior. In times of great pain and frustration, I have physically felt the weight of my burdens lift off my shoulders and be replaced with an inexplicable peace that is accompanied with the joy of knowing God has me in His hands. We were created to experience the joy of communion with God. Are you seeking the temporary "happiness" of this world, or are you seeking the eternal "joy" God desires for you?

The third way to maximize your joy is through fellowship with other believers. In 1 John 1:3–4, the apostle writes, "that which we have seen and heard we proclaim also to you, so that you too may have fellowship with us; and indeed our fellowship is with the Father and with his Son Jesus Christ. And we are writing these things so that our joy may be complete." John wanted the reader to understand it is important to have fellowship with one another. It lifts our spirits to be together and to hear how God is working in each other's lives. As believers, it is important to have other like-minded brothers and sisters in your life you can share with. Matthew 18:20 promises believers that when two or three gather in His name, God is among them. This does not mean believers' gatherings can only be somber occasions. Brothers and sisters, we should be showing the world how to be joyful. We have the only true source of joy. Our gatherings should be full of fun, laughter, and sharing. Godly friendships need to be a priority for us. Growing and fostering relationships with other believers will increase our joy.

The last way to maximize your joy is through giving. Two Corinthians 9:7 says, "Each one must give as he has decided in his heart, not reluctantly or under compulsion, for God loves a cheerful giver." You cannot out give God. Malachi 3:10 tells us, "'Bring the whole tithe into the storehouse, that there may be food in my house. Test me in this,' says the LORD Almighty, 'and see if I will not throw open the floodgates of heaven and pour out so much blessing that there will not be room enough to store it.'" At a time of year when our budgets are strained to the max, you may feel like you have nothing left to give. Remember when we talked about simplifying the holidays? Not only does that help you prepare your hearts by improving your ability to focus on what matters, it can increase your joy at Christmas. Who could you bless with the money you would save if you cut out three Starbucks visits this month? How much could you give to a family in need if everyone got four gifts this year instead of five? Giving is not just limited to the giving of material things. You can gain joy by giving to your family. Put your phone down and give them your full attention when they are talking to you. Ask questions when your friends share about their dreams or just how their day went. Give your time by being the first to take out the trash when you notice it is full instead of seeing how many more times you can jam something down in it before it explodes. Give love to those you call important in your life by pausing from your busy day to send them a text or phone call to tell them you are thinking of them and that you're praying for them. Do not get so busy this Christmas season that you forget to show the ways you love each other. There is inexplicable joy in the giving of ourselves and our resources.

Suggested Reading

Suggested Daily Readings

As you read, reflect on these questions: What is a situation you are trusting God with right now? How can you pray for those in your life? Make a plan to set aside time and have fun with your faith-based family. Do not forget to experience the joy God intended for you this Christmas season. Spend time reflecting over these verses and jot down notes in the space below. Earlier, you came up with a plan to stay intentionally focused on the true reason for Christmas. Take some time to check on your own progress. How are you doing? Are there areas where you need to improve?

Day 11—Psalm 146:1–10

_____

_____

_____

_____

_____

_____

_____

_____

_____

_____

_____

_____

_____

_____

_____

_____

Day 12—Luke 1:26–33

_____
_____
_____
_____
_____
_____
_____
_____
_____
_____
_____
_____
_____
_____
_____
_____
_____

Day 13—2 Corinthians 9:6–15

_____
_____
_____
_____
_____
_____
_____
_____
_____
_____
_____
_____
_____
_____
_____
_____
_____

Day 14—Philippians 4:4–13

_____
_____
_____
_____
_____
_____
_____
_____
_____
_____
_____
_____
_____
_____
_____
_____
_____

Day 15—Luke 2:7–15

_____
_____
_____
_____
_____
_____
_____
_____
_____
_____
_____
_____
_____
_____
_____
_____
_____
_____

Week 4

Love

Week 4

Love

Beloved, let us love one another, for love is from God, and whoever loves has been born of God and knows God. Anyone who does not love does not know God, because God is love. In this the love of God was made manifest among us, that God sent his only Son into the world, so that we might live through him.

—1 John 4:7–9

One of the very first Bible verses children learn in church today is John 3:16, which says, "For God so loved the world, that he gave his only Son, that whoever believes in him should not perish but have eternal life." The majority of believing adults know this verse, especially if they have spent any time in the church. Even many unbelieving adults have heard this verse; they've seen it on athletes' shoes or on the black markings under a football player's eyes. This verse has become so common it's now trite. We can mindlessly rattle it off but do we ever ponder it? Do we ever let the full impact of what Jesus is saying hit us? "For God so loved ..." The word "loved" here is translated to the Greek word *agapao*, which is a verb meaning to love, to take pleasure in; literally to have a preference for. This word *agapao* is used one hundred and forty-three times in the Bible, and twenty-seven times in the book of John alone. Jesus was telling the disciples that God so preferred *us* that He sent His only Son down to earth to live among us in our weak humanity, and ultimately, to die an excruciating and humiliating death. That, brothers and sisters, is how much God *preferred* you.

In John 13:34–35 Jesus, tells the disciples, "A new commandment I give to you, that you love one another: just as I have loved you, you also are to love one another. By this all people will know that you are my disciples, if you have love for one another." The biblical love Jesus is describing here is a sacrificial love. It puts others above itself. This kind of love does not make sense to the world. It is countercultural in every way; that's what makes it stand out so starkly in this cold and selfish world. "Just as I have loved you ..." How did Jesus love us? He loved us completely, unconditionally, and sacrificially. He loved us literally to death. What made the early church grow like wildfire was the presence of the Holy Spirit, of course, and an unexplained love between believers. The world saw how people from all different walks of life sold all they had and lived in peace together. People, who on paper should not get along, were not just civil to each other, but they *loved* one another. The world can't understand this, but when they see it, they know it has to be something special. We cannot love with this kind of love out of our own strength. Our sinful nature even fights against it. That is why we must study Jesus in the pages of scripture. Jesus did not just command us to love in this sacrificial way and tell us good luck! He lived this love out for us to read and model.

The New Testament uses the Greek word *splaghnizomai* (pronounced splang-nid-zom-ahee). It looks like a typo, but it's actually a verb meaning to have compassion. [6]Strong's concordance defines it as "to be moved to one's bowels [for the bowels were thought to be the seat of love and pity]." Isn't that a lovely mental picture? This word is used twelve times in the New Testament. It is the verb used in Luke 15:20 to describe what the father of the prodigal son felt when he saw his son walking up from the distance. It is also the verb used in Matthew 14:14, after Jesus heard about the beheading of His cousin, John the Baptist, and tried to withdraw. The people followed Him and he *splaghnizomai*, or was moved to compassion for them. Out of this loving compassion, He gave of Himself and healed

---

[6] Blue Letter Bible, https://www.blueletterbible.org/lexicon/g4697/kjv/tr/0-1.

JOY BANNEN

their sick. Furthermore, He proceeded to feed five thousand men and unknown thousands of women and children from just five loaves of bread and two fish. We cannot love others without compassion.

[7]In a sermon by Francis Chan, he references Colossians 3:12 "Therefore, as God's chosen people, holy and dearly loved, clothe yourselves with compassion, kindness, humility, gentleness and patience." Chan said, as he read that verse, he just stopped at the phrase "holy and dearly loved" and let that wash over him. The God of the universe completely and dearly loves him. He, a sinner who deserves death, is made holy by God. When we acknowledge the depth of God's love for us, it pours out of us in our compassion, our kindness, our gentleness, and our patience for one another. Jesus loved in a sacrificial way to bring all glory to God. We are able to love radically because "God so loved the world." We associate love with Valentine's Day, forgetting that the greatest act of love that moves us to love came in the form of a tiny baby. "God so loved the world that he gave his only Son." God so preferred a relationship with humanity that He sent His only Son down from heaven. What would you be willing to give up to better love another?

How Does This Apply to Our Relationships?

[8]In a sermon titled "Staying Married is Not About Staying in Love," John Piper made a strong statement about marriage, "marriage is the *display* of God. It is designed by God to display his glory in a way that no other event or institution is." If you have ever been in any type of relationship, you know love is not always easy. Love is a choice. We choose to love others by creating different types of human relationships. Love can be as simple as sacrificing your pick of a movie for one your friend will like. It can be putting on an extra sweater instead of turning up the heat because you know someone else in your house is always warm. Love can also be

---

[7] Francis Chan, "A New Attitude Towards People," 3/27/12, https://www.youtube.com/watch?v=_APxGs8wnM4.

[8] John Piper, "Staying Married is Not About Staying in Love," 1/28/07, https://www.desiringgod.org/messages/staying-married-is-not-about-staying-in-love.

as difficult as choosing to forgive and restore a relationship after a deep hurt. Love can be putting those hateful words said in anger in the past, leaving them there, and embracing the future together. This kind of love does not make sense. Our sinful nature tells us it is our right to be hurt and offended by others' insensitivity. Our sinful nature tells us we do not have to forgive our brother's or sister's betrayal. Sin tells us we can hold onto our anger and take care of ourselves because nobody else will. One Corinthians 13:4–7 has sadly become almost as trite as John 3:16 to believers and unbelievers alike who use this passage in weddings across America as a "nice reading." But in 1 Corinthians 13:4–7, Paul tells the church in Corinth the world is wrong about love. True love is not about what's fair; it's not self-seeking. Rather, Paul explains, "love is patient and kind; love does not envy or boast; it is not arrogant or rude. It does not insist on its own way; it is not irritable or resentful; it does not rejoice at wrongdoing, but rejoices with the truth. Love bears all things, believes all things, hopes all things, endures all things."

When I was researching the statistics on marriage, the ultimate human relationship model of Christ's love, these verses from 1 Corinthians kept coming to mind. Our marriages and families are falling apart because we are not willing to believe the best in each other, we are not willing to endure hard times, and instead, we are rude and arrogant. If we cannot be patient and graceful to our spouses who we claim to love, it makes sense that we are not patient in traffic, nor are we graceful when the restaurant messes up our order two times in a row. Our relationships are falling apart because we are trying to love out of our own strength, and not out of the abundance of love poured out from Christ.

God is very specific on what love is supposed to look like in our relationships with our fellow believers. Romans 12:9–21 is a clear guideline on what it looks like when the love of Christ comes out in our relationships. Specifically, verses 9–13 state, "Let love be genuine. Abhor what is evil; hold fast to what is good. Love one another with brotherly affection. Outdo one another in showing honor. Do not be slothful in zeal, be fervent in spirit, serve the Lord. Rejoice in hope, be patient in tribulation, be constant in prayer. Contribute to the needs of the saints and seek to show hospitality."

JOY BANNEN

Our love for one another should be genuine, not fake. We are to seek out opportunities to serve and honor one another, and not begrudgingly do so out of compulsion. The below verses are often the most difficult to apply in our lives.

> Bless those who persecute you; bless and do not curse them. Rejoice with those who rejoice, weep with those who weep. Live in harmony with one another. Do not be haughty, but associate with the lowly. Never be wise in your own sight. Repay no one evil for evil, but give thought to do what is honorable in the sight of all. If possible, so far as it depends on you, live peaceably with all. Beloved, never avenge yourselves, but leave it to the wrath of God, for it is written, "Vengeance is mine, I will repay, says the Lord." To the contrary, "if your enemy is hungry, feed him; if he is thirsty, give him something to drink; for by so doing you will heap burning coals on his head." Do not be overcome by evil, but overcome evil with good. (Romans 12:14–21)

The hurts we experience from a fellow believer, a member of our faith-based family, or a spiritual leader or mentor in our life are the sharpest and the hardest to process. When an unbeliever slanders against us, breaks a promise, or otherwise lets us down, we almost expect it and are able to work through that hurt. However, when a brother or sister in Christ wounds us, we feel justified to hold onto that pain, to tell others how we've been hurt (as a "prayer request"), to bring it to others attention because *someone* needs to know that person is not to be trusted. I have experienced this pain in my own life, this deep cut from a trusted fellow believer. I can attest to the difficulty it takes to process and move past the hurt; to continue serving alongside someone who betrayed the trust built between us. It took this passage in Romans (and *lots* of prayer) to remind me that vengeance is the Lord's. I am to be loving and not dwell on vengeance. Because of Christ's loving sacrifice on the cross, I can put my hurt in His hands and let Him intervene on my behalf. The hardest part of that passage for me was "so far as it depends on you, live peaceably with all." I didn't want to "live peaceably," I wanted justification to cut them out of my life. God showed me that I would not bring glory to Him by adding sin to an already broken situation. My obedience to Christ was simple: to love my brother and sister. As we talked about before, that love is not always easy. It goes past a simple feeling to an active choice made out of the abounding love of Christ in our lives. If we truly loved each other, as Christ continues to love us, our relationships would be radically changed. I want to wrap this section up with some words from my favorite Christmas carol, "O Holy Night."

> Truly He taught us to love one another
> His law is love and His gospel is peace
> Chains shall He break, for the slave is our brother
> And in His name, all oppression shall cease
> Sweet hymns of joy in grateful chorus raise we
> Let all within us praise His holy name

Suggested Reading

Suggested Daily Readings

As you read, reflect on these questions: Are you intentionally seeking to love others the way Christ loves you? Is your focus on material things and temporary pleasures, or is it on the immeasurable love of our Savior? Do your relationships reflect the love Christ has for the church as described in Romans 12:9–21? Spend time reflecting on these verses and jot down notes in the space below. Over the next few days, take some time to write two letters. One letter for someone in your life who has been there for you, but who you have not expressed your gratitude to yet. Thank them for the sacrifices they've made to show their love for you, and express your love and appreciation for them. The second letter is to God, thanking Him for His love in your life. Write out all the ways you have seen His hand in your life in the past year and in your relationships. Thank Him for His provision and grace.

Day 16—Lamentations 3:22–33

_____
_____
_____
_____
_____
_____
_____
_____
_____
_____
_____
_____
_____
_____
_____
_____

Day 17—Philippians 2:1–11

_____
_____
_____
_____
_____
_____
_____
_____
_____
_____
_____
_____
_____
_____
_____
_____
_____

Day 18—Ephesians 5:1–21

_____
_____
_____
_____
_____
_____
_____
_____
_____
_____
_____
_____
_____
_____
_____
_____
_____

Day 19—John 15:9–17

_____
_____
_____
_____
_____
_____
_____
_____
_____
_____
_____
_____
_____
_____
_____
_____

Day 20—1 John 4:7–21

_____
_____
_____
_____
_____
_____
_____
_____
_____
_____
_____
_____
_____
_____
_____
_____

Week 5

Christ

Week 5

Christ

And Joseph also went up from Galilee, from the town of Nazareth, to Judea, to the city of David, which is called Bethlehem, because he was of the house and lineage of David, to be registered with Mary, his betrothed, who was with child. And while they were there, the time came for her to give birth. And she gave birth to her firstborn son and wrapped him in swaddling cloths and laid him in a manger, because there was no place for them in the inn.

—Luke 2:4–7

This was not the first-time birth experience Mary was hoping to have. I have not asked her, but I can promise you, taking a sixty-plus-mile trip by donkey to Bethlehem a week before her due date is not any woman's idea of an ideal birth plan. Having to give birth either out in the elements or in a stable with most likely very limited privacy, then having only strips of cloth to keep her baby warm was most likely not what Mary had in mind when she had pondered giving birth to this holy child of God. Surely this miraculous Son of the Most High, whom an angel of God told her she carried, would have a more dignified birth. I have loved studying the story of Jesus's birth in Luke's account. It is so succinct, yet says so much.

The fact that Jesus was born through such a lowly, humble birth, with not so much as a fully woven blanket to cover Him, crushes my arrogance and entitlement. The fact that His first visitors were lowly shepherds who were looked down upon by society destroys any sense of indignation I am tempted to feel. My heart is so warmed by the beautiful symbolism God orchestrated by having inferior shepherds coming to visit the "Good Shepherd." A group of humble shepherds coming to visit the holy Lamb of God. [9]In "The Birth of the Messiah," Bob Deffinbaugh writes, "What had once appeared to be only a sequence of unfortunate events, now is revealed to be the hand of God working through history to accomplish God's will." If Mary can graciously endure such miserable circumstances through faith, how much more should I endure the minor inconveniences of life today? Mary's focus was fully on Christ—the beautiful, exciting, miraculous coming of Christ.

As we wrap up this time together in anticipation of Christmas, let's pause and reflect on who Jesus Christ is. The Bible is crystal clear on who Jesus is. Let's dig into to God's Word together. Acts 4:12 says, "And there is salvation in no one else, for there is no other name under heaven given among men by which we must be saved." Jesus is the only name that saves. One Peter 2:6 says, "Behold, I am laying in Zion a stone, a cornerstone chosen and precious, and whoever believes in him will not be put to shame." Jesus is our cornerstone, the very thing on which our salvation depends on. Revelation 7:17 says, "For the Lamb in the midst of the throne will be their shepherd, and he will guide them to springs of living water, and God will wipe away every tear from their eyes." Jesus is our good shepherd who will guide us to everlasting life where there will be no more tears, no more death, no more suffering. Revelation 1:17b–18 says, "Fear not, I am the first and the last, and the living one. I died, and behold I am alive forevermore, and I have the keys of Death and Hades." Then, Revelation 21:6 says, "I am the Alpha and the Omega, the beginning and the end." Jesus is the creator of time. He is beyond time. Life, death, and time answer to Him. The day is coming when He will unlock death and Hades and the final judgement will be upon us. One John 2:1 says, "But if anyone does sin, we have an advocate with the Father, Jesus Christ the

---

[9] Bob Deffinbaugh, "The Birth of the Messiah," 6/22/04, https://bible.org/seriespage/4-birth-messiah-luke-21-20.

righteous." Jesus is our advocate. When we struggle, when we fall, Jesus is our advocate, picking us up and saying, "It's OK, I've got this covered under my blood." When we should be condemned by our greed, our deceit, our irreverent tongues, Jesus stands between us and hell, and says, "That is my child!"

John 8:12 says, "Again Jesus spoke to them, saying, 'I am the light of the world. Whoever follows me will not walk in darkness, but will have the light of life.'" Jesus is the light of the world. He came down to earth to light our path to Him. We were lost, wandering around in the circles of our own sin and ugliness, until Jesus came to earth to direct our steps. When we accept Jesus into our hearts, His light fills us. We are able to shine His light on others, pointing them to Jesus. We are called to shine the light of His grace, His love, His kindness, and His truth to the world. We are also to shine this light in our relationships.

How Does This Apply to Our Lives?

Jesus is to be our first love, the most important figure in our lives. But this is where many of us get it wrong; we place everyone else in our lives before Jesus. There are several gray areas in the Bible that we may sometimes wish were spelled out for us, but this is not one of those areas. The scripture is consistently clear on this. Matthew 10:37 says, "Whoever loves father or mother more than me is not worthy of me, and whoever loves son or daughter more than me is not worthy of me." Matthew 22:36–38 says, "'Teacher, which is the great commandment in the Law?' And he said to him, 'You shall love the Lord your God with all your heart and with all your soul and with all your mind. This is the great and first commandment...'" Jesus, Himself, makes it perfectly clear that our first love should be for Him. We are to love Jesus more than our spouses, children, or parents. More than anything and anyone else in our lives. But what does that look like in our day-to-day lives?

Women shine the light of Jesus in their marriages when they show respect to and submit to their husbands. When you call your husband during his lunch break to update him on the Christmas plans, do not be so easily offended when he sounds hurried or distracted on the phone. Believe the best in him; that he loves you and would love to chat with you if he could, but work may be particularly stressful at that moment. Choose to believe his tone is not frustration with you, but perhaps with the situation he is facing at work. Men shine the light of Jesus in their marriages when they love and cherish their wives. When you've had a long frustrating day at work and your wife asks if you have asked your boss for the days before Christmas off yet, do not blow your stack at her for "nagging you." Love her and be patient with her, understand that she is only asking because she loves you and is looking forward to having you home a couple extra days. Colossians 3:22 says, "Fathers, do not provoke your children, lest they become discouraged." Parents, when your children are frantically searching for their homework before going to school and you ask if they've checked the kitchen, and they answer in a hurried affirmative, do not ask them a second time in a demeaning and unhelpful way. When you have plans with a friend who has to cancel at the last minute, rather than taking the change in plans personally, seek to understand what is going on in your friend's life. Rather than being annoyed and hurt by your friend, pray for them. Ask if there is anything you can do to help them. Christ was so unendingly patient and compassionate with humans. He did not berate people for doubting or not understanding right away. He did not take a deep sigh and roll His eyes as His very own disciples failed to understand what He was teaching. When the disciples did fall and mess up, Jesus did not demean them. He did not raise His voice to them. He did not tell them that to be His disciples they must perform perfectly according to His standards and make Him proud. He did not seek to control them, but to serve them graciously. Likewise, we are called to be gracious, loving, and serving to one another as fellow image bearers. So many of the conflicts we have with one another could be avoided. When we choose to believe the best in each other and gracefully overlook the small things, we open the door to more love, which builds respect. Let the love and light of Christ shine out to the world through our relationships. Matthew 5:16 tells us, "In the same way, let your light shine before others, that they may see your good deeds and glorify your Father in heaven."

JOY BANNEN

Suggested Reading

Suggested Daily Readings

As you read, reflect on these questions: Is there a situation you are facing that, from the outside, appears to be a series of unfortunate events? Who could you share with to help you look to the attributes of Christ to get you through this time? Are you living a life that excitedly anticipates the Second Coming of Christ? If you truly believe Jesus is coming on January 1, what will you change? Check in with those close around you, is there a way you can help encourage them? A way you can serve them as their helper? What can you do to better shine the light of Christ to those God has placed in your life? You cannot change others, but you can change *you*. Reflect on these verses and jot down notes in the space below.

Day 21—Psalm 96:1–13

_____
_____
_____
_____
_____
_____
_____
_____
_____
_____
_____
_____
_____
_____
_____
_____
_____

Day 22—Isaiah 9:1–7

_____
_____
_____
_____
_____
_____
_____
_____
_____
_____
_____
_____
_____
_____
_____
_____

Day 23—Psalm 98:1–9

_____
_____
_____
_____
_____
_____
_____
_____
_____
_____
_____
_____
_____
_____
_____
_____
_____

Day 24—Ezekiel 1:4–28

_____
_____
_____
_____
_____
_____
_____
_____
_____
_____
_____
_____
_____
_____
_____
_____
_____

Day 25—Revelations 22:6–21

_____
_____
_____
_____
_____
_____
_____
_____
_____
_____
_____
_____
_____
_____
_____
_____
_____
_____

Fear not, for behold, I bring you good news of great joy
that will be for all the people. For unto you is born this
day in the city of David a Savior, who is Christ the Lord.
(Luke 2:10–11)

Final Thoughts

And you, child, will be called the prophet of the Most High; for you will go before the Lord to prepare his ways, to give knowledge of salvation to his people in the forgiveness of their sins, because of the tender mercy of our God, whereby the sunrise shall visit us from on high to give light to those who sit in darkness and in the shadow of death, to guide our feet into the way of peace.

—Luke 1:76–79

Until my time studying the Advent, I had not connected the significance of John the Baptist with Christmas. John the Baptist is mentioned in all of the gospels, but I had never contemplated the historical importance of John's ministry. He plays such a vital role in the unique circumstances surrounding the coming Christ. John the Baptist joined an esteemed line of proclaimers of Advent before we had a name for it, yet the timing of his message stands out among the other prophets' messages. When other prophets proclaimed the coming Christ, they were speaking of a time hundreds of years into the future. When John the Baptist proclaimed the coming of Christ, he was talking to that current generation. His message had an urgency to it Israel had not heard in quite some time. When John the Baptist was born, there had been no prophets in Israel for hundreds of years. The Bible prophesied about the coming of this final prophet:

A voice cries: "In the wilderness prepare the way of the LORD; make straight in the desert a highway for our God. Every valley shall be lifted up, and every mountain and hill be made low; the uneven ground shall become level, and the rough places a plain. And the glory of the LORD shall be revealed, and all flesh shall see it together, for the mouth of the LORD has spoken." (Isaiah 40:3–5)

John the Baptist called the people to repent and be baptized to prepare themselves for the coming of the Messiah. Mark 1:3 says, "...'Prepare the way of the Lord, make his paths straight.'" John the Baptist is significant, not because he was Jesus's cousin, not because he had a miraculous birth to elderly parents, and not because an angel announced his birth; John the Baptist is significant because of his message. Matthew 3:1–2 says, "In those days John the Baptist came preaching in the wilderness of Judea, 'Repent, for the kingdom of heaven is at hand.'" While Mark 1:7 says, "After me comes he who is mightier than I, the strap of whose sandals I am not worthy to stoop down and untie." John prophesied the coming of Christ and called for Israel to spiritually prepare itself for the coming holy King.

During this season of Advent, do you find yourself feeling spiritually unprepared for Christ's Second Coming? Remember the steps we discussed these past twenty-five days.

- **Reflect.** Spend time in honest, somber self-reflection. Psalm 139:23 says, "Search me, O God, and know my heart; Try me and know my anxious thoughts." What distractions are in your life or in your schedule that are taking your focus off Christ? What changes can you make? What has God done in and through your life that you can praise Him for? Reflect on this past year, be honest with yourself when assessing how you have handled the stress and frustration of life's earthly situations. One Chronicles 28:9 says, " ...for the LORD searches all hearts, and understands every intent of the thoughts If you seek Him, He will let you find Him ..." Ask God to reveal to you any areas that need pruning or fine-tuning. Talk to those who are close to you; ask if there are ways you can better serve them. Are you loving them, not how you would want to be loved, but how *they* need to be loved?

- **Spend time in the Word.** This cannot be emphasized enough. The phrase "read your Bible" has become as trite an answer to believers as "Jesus" is to Sunday school questions. However, Revelation 1:3 says, "Blessed is the one who reads aloud the words of this prophecy, and blessed are those who hear, and who keep what is written in it, for the time is near." We cannot prepare ourselves for the coming of someone we do not know. The only way to get to know Christ is through studying His words and the words of His closest apostles, which are recorded in the Bible. Read scripture, meditate on His Word, and memorize it. If you are someone who has always struggled with reading the Bible, ask God to give you a thirst for His Word. Ask someone you trust to help keep you accountable. Make your time with His Word the focus of your day, not the thing you squeeze in when you can. Cut something out of your schedule if needed. There is literally nothing that is more important for you to give your time to each day. Let the scripture listed in this devotional be the starting point of your journey to devoting more time to studying God's Word.
- **Dedicate yourselves to prayer.** Reading the Word of God gives us knowledge about Christ our Redeemer, but prayer is our direct line of communication with Him. Do not forget that, as part of His new covenant with us, we can now pray to Jesus freely without a priest to speak for us. Jeremiah 29:12 says, "Then you will call upon me and come and pray to me, and I will hear you." While Psalm 145:18 says, "The LORD is near to all who call on him, to all who call on him in truth." In your prayers, do not mindlessly list all the things you need or want, do not list the situations you want changed. I once heard a pastor say, "If God were to answer all of your prayers today, would anyone's life change besides your own?" You have a direct line to God. Who are you praying for? Pray for your friends; pray that God will grow them and give them a thirst for Him. Pray for your family members and children; pray that God will lead them and draw them near. Pray for your unsaved coworkers; pray that they can come to know the saving grace of Jesus Christ, and that He will

use you as His vessel. Pray for those who are away from family this year, either loved ones departed or estranged relationships; pray that they will feel God's presence near them. Pray that God will radically change your view of Him, and that He will set you on fire for Him. Pray that you can be a willing servant, and can encourage your brothers and sisters along the way.

Life on this earth can be painful. It can be tough, it can be difficult, and it can get ugly. Believers persevere in the knowledge that the only one who can take away the sins of the world is coming back soon! Like a thief in the night, He will appear and bring us home with Him. When blessings fall on us, they are reminders that God is looking down on us, and He loves us. It is for this reason that I love rainbows. As a child, every time I saw a rainbow I would think God was winking at me. I am constantly amazed at the beauty of sunrises and sunsets. The swirls of colors make me think of the myriad of colors we will see in heaven. I imagine walking on the glassy sky-like streets of heaven. We can persevere because we know our trials here are momentary; our reward in heaven with our Savior will be forever. Never forget that our Savior is parousia. He is coming again. New Testament believers who saw Jesus ascend into the clouds literally lived life with their eyes on the skies with the expectation of Christ's return. Where are you looking? To the things of the world around you, or to the sky, expecting our Savior? At this time, when the world calls you to focus on material and temporary things, remember Jesus's promise:

> Let not your hearts be troubled. Believe in God; believe also in me. In my Father's house are many rooms. If it were not so, would I have told you that I go to prepare a place for you? And if I go and prepare a place for you, I will come again and will take you to myself, that where I am you may be also. (John 14:1-3)

Praise the Lord! Jesus has come, and He is coming again! I want to end this time with the words of another favorite Christmas carol as sung by [10]Casting Crowns, "O Come, O Come, Emmanuel."

O come, O come, Emmanuel
And ransom captive Israel
That mourns in lonely exile here
Until the Son of God appear
Rejoice, rejoice, Emmanuel
Shall come to thee, O Israel

O come, Thou Rod of Jesse, free
Thine own from Satan's tyranny
From depths of Hell Thy people save
And give them victory o'er the grave
Rejoice, rejoice, Emmanuel
Shall come to thee, o Israel

O come, Thou Day-Spring
Come and cheer
Our spirits by Thine advent here
Disperse the gloomy clouds of night
And death's dark shadows put to flight
Rejoice, rejoice, Emmanuel
Shall come to thee, o Israel

O come, Thou Key of David, come
And open wide our heavenly home
Make safe the way that leads on high
And close the path to misery
Rejoice, rejoice, Emmanuel
Shall come to thee, o Israel

[10] Casting Crowns, *O Come, O Come, Emmanuel*, 2008, https://genius.com/Casting-crowns-o-come-o-come-emmanuel-lyrics.

O come, O come, Thou Lord of might
Who to Thy tribes, on Sinai's height
In ancient times did'st give the Law
In cloud, and majesty and awe
Rejoice, rejoice, Emmanuel
Shall come to thee, o Israel

Printed in the United States
by Baker & Taylor Publisher Services